A NEW YORK SHAKESPEARE FESTIVAL PRODUCTION
in association with **Plum Productions**

Joseph Papp
Presents

A CHORUS LINE

Conceived, Choreographed and Directed by
Michael Bennett

Book by	Music by	Lyrics by
James Kirkwood &	**Marvin Hamlisch**	**Edward Kleban**
Nicholas Dante		

Co-choreographer
Bob Avian

with (in alphabetical order)

Scott Allen	Renee Baughman	Carole Bishop	Pamela Blair
Wayne Cilento	Chuck Cissel	Clive Clerk	Kay Cole
Ronald Dennis	Donna Drake	Brandt Edwards	Patricia Garland
Carolyn Kirsch	Ron Kuhlman	Nancy Lane	Baayork Lee
Priscilla Lopez	Robert LuPone	Cameron Mason	Donna McKechnie
Don Percassi	Carole Schweid	Michael Serrecchia	Michel Stuart
Thomas J. Walsh	Sammy Williams	Crissy Wilzak	

Setting by	Costumes by	Lighting by
Robin Wagner	**Theoni V. Aldredge**	**Tharon Musser**

Orchestrations by	Music Coordinator
Bill Byers, Hershy Kay &	**Robert Thomas**
Jonathan Tunick	

Music Direction and Vocal Arrangements by
Don Pippin

Associate Producer
Bernard Gersten

Produced for records by
Goddard Lieberson

Applications for performance of this work, whether legitimate, stock,
amateur, or foreign, should be addressed to:
TAMS-WITMARK
560 Lexington Avenue
New York, NY 10022

Published by
MPL COMMUNICATIONS, INC.

Exclusively distributed by
HAL LEONARD PUBLISHING CORPORATION
Winona, MN 55987   Milwaukee, WI 53213

A CHORUS LINE

CONTENTS

Piano/Vocal Section

Lead Line Section

Cover: Courtesy of COLUMBIA RECORDS

Published by
MPL COMMUNICATIONS, INC.

Exclusively distributed by

HAL LEONARD PUBLISHING CORPORATION

Winona, MN 55987   Milwaukee, WI 53213

I HOPE I GET IT

Music by **MARVIN HAMLISCH**
Lyric by **EDWARD KLEBAN**

(All:) God, I hope I get it,

I hope I get it. How man - y peo - ple does he need?

(Boys:) How man - y peo - ple does he

(All:) God, I real-ly blew it! I real-ly blew it. How could I do a thing like

Alright, let me see the boys. The whole group.   *Ready, 5, 6, 7, 8!*

I CAN DO THAT

Music by **MARVIN HAMLISCH**
Lyric by **EDWARD KLEBAN**

24

(now mar - ried and fat)   I can do this.

taps cadenza

f

That I can do,—

N.C.   I can do that.—

AT THE BALLET

Music by MARVIN HAMLISCH
Lyric by EDWARD KLEBAN

Intense, emotional, driving

though she was twen - ty - two, — though she was twen - ty - two, _____ she

mar - ried him. _____ Life with my dad was-n't ev - er a pic-nic.

More like a "Come as you are." _____ When I was five I re -

mem - ber my moth - er dug ear - rings out of the car. _____

SING!

♩ notes—person who can't sing
♪ notes—person who can

Music by **MARVIN HAMLISCH**
Lyric by **EDWARD KLEBAN**

HELLO TWELVE, HELLO THIRTEEN, HELLO LOVE

Music by **MARVIN HAMLISCH**
Lyric by **EDWARD KLEBAN**

41

NOTHING

Music by **MARVIN HAMLISCH**
Lyric by **EDWARD KLEBAN**

I'm so excited because I'm gonna go to the High School of Performing Arts.
I mean, I was dying to be a serious actress. Anyway it's the first day
of acting class and we're in the auditorium and the teacher, Mister Karp,
puts us up on the stage with our legs around everybody, one in back of
the other, and he says: O.K., we're gonna do improvisations. Now, you're
on a bobsled and it's snowing out and it's cold. O. K., go!

Light Rock   *(Repeat as needed under spoken introduction)*

Ev - 'ry - day   for a   week we would try to   feel   the   mo - tion,
Sec - ond week,   more ad - vanced and we   had to   be   a   ta - ble,

feel   the   mo - tion   down the   hill. _____
be   a   sports car...   ice cream cone. _____

44

I'm feel - ing noth-ing," _____ and he says, "Noth-ing could

get a girl trans - fered." They all felt some-thing, ____

but I felt noth-ing _____ ex - cept the feel - ing that this

bull - shit was ab - surd! *But I said to myself, "Hey! it's*

46

48

THE MUSIC AND THE MIRROR

Music by **MARVIN HAMLISCH**
Lyric by **EDWARD KLEBAN**

53

DANCE: TEN; LOOKS: THREE

Music by **MARVIN HAMLISCH**
Lyric by **EDWARD KLEBAN**

62

ONE

Music by **MARVIN HAMLISCH**
Lyric by **EDWARD KLEBAN**

Give her your at-ten-tion. Do I real-ly have to men-tion,

she's the one?

She walks in-to a room___ and you know___ she's un-

com-mon-ly rare, ver-y u-nique, per-i-pa-tet-ic, po-et-ic and chic.

68

WHAT I DID FOR LOVE

Music by **MARVIN HAMLISCH**
Lyric by **EDWARD KLEBAN**

77

James Kirkwood   Edward Kleban   Marvin Hamlisch
                     Michael Bennett   Nicholas Dante

Music by Marvin Hamlisch

Lyrics by Edward Kleban

A CHORUS LINE

I HOPE I GET IT
By Marvin Hamlisch and Edward Kleban

(Zach:) Again! Step, kick, kick, leap, kick, touch.
Again! Step, kick, kick, leap, kick, touch.
Again! Step, kick, kick, leap, kick, touch.
Again! Step, kick, kick, leap, kick, touch.
Right! That connects with turn, turn out, in touch, step,
Step, kick, kick, leap, kick, touch.
Got it? Going on and turn, turn, touch down,
Back step, pivot step, walk, walk, walk. Right!
Let's do the whole combination facing away from the mirror.
From the top! 5, 6, 7, 8!
(All:) God, I hope I get it, I hope I get it.
How many people does he need?
(Boys:) How many people does he need?
(All:) God, I hope I get it. I hope I get it.
How many boys, how many
(Boys:) girls?
(Girls:) How many boys, how many . .?
(Boys:) Look at all the people! . . . At all the people.
How many people does he need?
How many boys? How many girls?
How many people does he . . .?
(Solo:) I really need this job.
Please, God, I need this job.
I've got to get this job!
(Zach:) Stage left, boys.
Let's do the ballet combination,
First group of girls, second group to follow.
1, 2, 3, 4, 5, 6.
(All:) God, I really blew it! I really blew it.
How could I do a thing like that?
How could I do a thing like . . .?
Now, I'll never make it! I'll never make it!
He doesn't like the way I look.
He doesn't like the way I dance.
He doesn't like the way I . . .
(Zach:) Alright, let me see the boys.
The whole group. Ready, 5, 6, 7, 8!
Okay, Girls, 5, 6, 7, 8!
(Group:) God, I think I've got it.
I think I've got it. I knew he liked me all the time.
Still, it isn't over. It isn't over.
I can't imagine what he wants. I can't imagine what he . . .
God, I hope I get it! I hope I get it.
I've come this far, but even so:
It could be yes, it could be no.
How many people does he . .?
(Others:) I really need this job.
Please, God, I need this job.
(All:) I've got to get this show.
(Paul:) Who am I anyway? Am I my resume?
That is a picture of a person I don't know.
What does he want from me?
What should I try to be?
So many faces all around, and here we go.
I need this job. Oh God, I need this show.

I CAN DO THAT

By Marvin Hamlisch and Edward Kleban

I'm watchin' Sis go pit-a-pat,
Said, I can do that, I can do that.
Knew ev'ry step right off the bat,
Said, I can do that, I can do that.
One morning Sis won't go to dance class,
I grab her shoes and tights and all,
But my foot's too small, so,
I stuff her shoes with extra socks,
Run seven blocks in nothin' flat,
Hell, I can do that, I can do that.
I got to class and had it made,
And so I stayed the rest of my life.
All thanks to Sis, (now married and fat)
I can do this.
That I can do, I can do that.

AT THE BALLET

By Marvin Hamlisch and Edward Kleban

Daddy always thought that he married beneath him,
That's what he said, that's what he said.
When he proposed he informed my mother
He was probably her very last chance.
And though she was twenty-two, though she was twenty-two,
Though she was twenty-two, she married him.
Life with my dad wasn't ever a picnic,
More like a "Come as you are."
When I was five I remember my mother
Dug earrings out of the car.
I knew they weren't hers, but it wasn't something
You'd wanna discuss.
He wasn't warm, *well, not to her. . . well, not to us!*
But ev'rything was beautiful at the ballet.
Graceful men lift lovely girls in white.
Yes, ev'rything was beautiful at the ballet,
Hey! I was happy at the ballet.
Up a steep and very narrow stairway to the voice like a metronome.
Up a steep and very narrow stairway, it wasn't Paradise,
It wasn't Paradise, it wasn't Paradise, but it was home.
Mother always said I'd be very attractive
When I grew up, when I grew up.
"Diff'rent", she said, "With a special something
And a very, very personal flair."
And though I was eight or nine, though I was eight or nine,
Though I was eight or nine, I hated her.
Now "diff'rent" is nice, but it sure isn't pretty.
"Pretty" is what it's about.
I never met anyone who was "diff'rent"
Who couldn't figure that out.
So beautiful I'd never live to see.
But it was clear, *if not to her, well, then to me!*
That ev'ryone is beautiful at the ballet.
Ev'ry prince has got to have his swan.
Yes, ev'ryone is beautiful at the ballet,
Hey! I was pretty at the ballet.
Up a steep and very narrow stairway to the voice like a metronome.
Up a steep and very narrow stairway, it wasn't Paradise,
It wasn't Paradise, it wasn't Paradise, but it was home.
Ev'rything was beautiful at the ballet.
Raise your arms and someone's always there.
Yes, ev'rything was beautiful at the ballet,
Hey! I was pretty, I was happy,
"I would love to" . . . At the ballet.

SING!
By Marvin Hamlisch and Edward Kleban

See, I really couldn't sing. *I could never really* sing.
What I couldn't do was sing.
I have trouble with a note. *It goes all around my* throat.
It's a terrifying thing.
See, I really couldn't hear which note was lower or was higher.
Which is why I disappear if someone says "Let's start a choir."
Hey, when I begin to shriek, *it's a cross between a* squeak
And a quiver or a moan.
It's a little like a croak *or the record player* broke.
What it doesn't have is tone.
Oh, I know you're thinking what a crazy ding-a-ling.
But I really couldn't sing. *I could never really* sing.
What I couldn't do was sing!
Three blind mice, *Three blind mice, it isn't intentional.*
(She's doing her best.*)*
Jingle Bells, Jingle Bells. *Jingle Bells, Jingle Bells, it really blows my mind.*
(She gets depressed.*)*
But what I lack in pitch I sure make up in power!
And all my friends say I am perfect for the shower.
Still, I'm terrific at a dance. *Guys are comin' in their* pants.
I'm a birdie on the wing.
But when I begin to chirp, *they say "Who's the little* twerp
*Goin' 'pong' instead of '*ping*'?"*
And when Christmas comes and all my friends go caroling,
*It is so dishearten-*ning. *It is so disquiet-*ting.
*It is so discourag-*ging, *darling, please stop answer-*ring.
See I really couldn't sing. *I could never really* sing.
What I couldn't do was sing!

HELLO TWELVE, HELLO THIRTEEN, HELLO LOVE
By Marvin Hamlisch and Edward Kleban

Hello Twelve, Hello Thirteen, Hello Love.
Changes, Oh! down below, up above.
Time to doubt, to break out, it's a mess.
(It's a mess.)
Time to grow, time to go adolesce.
(Adolesce.)
Too young to take over, too old to ignore.
Gee, I'm almost ready, *but what for?*
There's a lot I am not certain of.
Hello Twelve, Hello Thirteen, Hello Love.

NOTHING
By Marvin Hamlisch and Edward Kleban

Ev'ryday for a week we would try to feel the motion,
Feel the motion down the hill.
Ev'ryday day for a week we would try to hear the wind rush,
Hear the wind rush, feel the chill.
And I dug right down to the bottom of my soul to see
What I had inside.
Yes, I dug right down to the bottom of my soul and I tried,
I tried.
And everybody's going Woosh . . . . woosh . . . . . .
I feel the snow, I feel the cold . . . I feel the air."
And Mr. Karp turns to me and he says,
"O.K., Morales, what did you feel?"
And I said, "Nothing, I'm feeling nothing,"
And he says, "Nothing could get a girl transfered."
They all felt something, but I felt nothing
Except the feeling that this bull-shit was absurd!
But, I said to myself, "Hey! it's only the first week.
Maybe it's genetic, they don't have bobsleds in San Juan!"
Second week, more advanced and we had to be a table,
Be a sports car . . . ice cream cone.
Mister Karp, he would say, "Very good, except Morales.
Try, Morales, all alone."
So I dug right down to the bottom of my soul to see
How an ice cream felt.

Yes, I dug right down to the bottom of my soul and I tried
To melt.
The kids yelled "Nothing!" They called me "Nothing"
And Karp allowed it, which really makes me burn.
They were so helpful, they called me "Hopeless",
Until I really didn't know where else to turn.
And Karp kept saying,
"Morales, I think you should transfer to Girl's High . . .
You'll never be an actress. Never!" Jesus Christ!
Went to church, praying, Santa Maria, send me guidance,
Send me guidance on my knees.
Went to church, praying, Santa Maria, help me feel it,
Help me feel it, pretty please.
And a voice from down at the bottom of my soul came up
To the top of my head,
And the voice from down at the bottom of my soul,
Here is what it said:
This man is nothing, this course is nothing,
If you want something, go find another class.
And when you find one you'll be an actress.
And I assure you that's what fin'lly came to pass.
Six months later I heard that Karp had died.
And I dug right down to the bottom of my soul . . . and cried
'Cause I felt nothing.

DANCE: TEN; LOOKS: THREE
By Marvin Hamlisch and Edward Kleban

Dance: Ten; Looks: Three
And I'm still on unemployment,
Dancing for my own enjoyment.
That ain't it, kid! That ain't it, kid!
Dance: Ten; Looks: Three is like to die.
Left the the'ter and called the doctor
For my appointment to buy . . .
Tits and ass. Bought myself a fancy pair.
Tightened up the derriere.
Did the nose with it, all that goes with it.
Tits and ass! Had the bingo-bongos done.
Suddenly I'm getting Nash'nal tours!
Tits and ass won't get you jobs,
Unless they're yours.
Didn't cost a fortune, neither.
Didn't hurt my sex life, either.
Flat and sassy, I would get the strays and losers,
Beggars really can't be choosers.
That ain't it, kid! That ain't it, kid!

Fixed the chassis, "How do you do!"
Life turned into an endless medley of
"Gee, it had to be you." *Why?*
Tits and ass. Where the cupboard once was bare,
Now you knock and someone's there.
You have got 'em, hey! Top to bottom, hey!
It's a gas! Just a dash of silicone.
Shake your new maracas and you're fine!
Tits and ass can change your life,
They sure changed mine.
Have it all done. Honey, take my word.
Grab a cab, c'mon, see the wizard on Park and Seventy Third
For tits and ass. Orchestra and balcony.
What they want is what cha see.
Keep the best of you, do the rest of you.
Pits or class, I have never seen it fail,
Debutante or chorus girl or wife.
Tits and ass, yes, tits and ass have changed my life.

THE MUSIC AND THE MIRROR
By Marvin Hamlisch and Edward Kleban

Give me somebody to dance for.
Give me somebody to show.
Let me wake up in the morning to find
I have somewhere exciting to go.
To have something that I can believe in,
To have someone to be.
Use me, choose me,
God, I'm a dancer, a dancer dances!
Give me somebody to dance with.
Give me a place to fit in.
Help me return to the world of the living
By showing me how to begin.
Play me the music, give me a chance to come through.
All I ever needed was the music and the mirror
And the chance to dance for you.
Give me a job and you instantly get me involved.
If you give me a job then the rest
Of the crap will get solved.
Put me to work, you would think that by now I'm allowed.
I'll do you proud.
Throw me a rope to grab on to,
Help me to prove that I'm strong.
Give me the chance to look forward to sayin'
"Hey, listen they're playin' my song."
Play me the music, play me the music,
Play me the music.
Give me a chance to come through.
All I ever needed was the music
And the mirror and the chance to dance for you.

WHAT I DID FOR LOVE
By Marvin Hamlisch and Edward Kleban

Kiss today good-bye,
The sweetness and the sorrow.
We did what we had to do,
And I can't regret
What I did for love;
What I did for love.
Look, my eyes are dry,
The gift was ours to borrow.
It's as if we always knew,
But I won't forget what I did for love;
What I did for love.
Gone, love is never gone,
As we travel on,
Love's what we'll remember.
Kiss today good-bye,
And point me t'ward tomorrow.
Wish me luck; the same to you.
Won't forget, can't regret
What I did for love.
What I did for love.
What I did for love.

ONE
By Marvin Hamlisch and Edward Kleban

One singular sensation ev'ry little step she takes.
One thrilling combination ev'ry move that she makes.
One smile and suddenly nobody else will do.
You know you'll never be lonely with you-know-who.
One moment in her presence and you can forget the rest,
For the girl is second best to none, son.
Ooooh! Sigh! Give her your attention.
Do I really have to mention, she's the one?
She walks into a room and you know
She's uncommonly rare, very unique, peripatetic,
Poetic and chic.
She walks into a room and you know
From her maddening poise, effortless whirl,
She's the special girl strolling,
Can't help all of her qualities extolling.

Loaded with charisma is ma jauntily,
Sauntering, ambling, shambler.
She walks into a room and you know
You must shuffle along, join the parade.
She's the quintessence of making the grade.
This is whatcha call trav'lling!
Oh, strut your stuff. Can't get enough of her.
Love her. I'm a son of a gun, she is one of a kind.
One singular sensation ev'ry little step she takes.
One thrilling combination ev'ry move that she makes.
One smile and suddenly nobody else will do.
You know you'll never be lonely with you-know-who.
One moment in her presence and you can forget the rest,
For the girl is second best to none, son.
Ooooh! Sigh! Give her your attention.
Do I really have to mention, she's the one?

I HOPE I GET IT
From the Joseph Papp production of Michael Bennett's "A CHORUS LINE"

Lyric by EDWARD KLEBAN
Music by MARVIN HAMLISCH

I CAN DO THAT
From the Joseph Papp production of Michael Bennett's "A CHORUS LINE"

Lyric by EDWARD KLEBAN
Music by MARVIN HAMLISCH

AT THE BALLET *From the Joseph Papp Production of Michael Bennett's "A CHORUS LINE"*

Music by MARVIN HAMLISCH
Lyric by EDWARD KLEBAN

Intense, emotional, driving

Dad-dy al-ways thought that he mar-ried be-neath him, that's what he said, that's what he said. When he pro-posed he in-formed my moth-er he was prob-a-bly her ver-y last chance. And though she was twen-ty-two, though she was twen-ty-two, though she was twen-ty-two, she mar-ried him. Life with my dad was-n't ev-er a pic-nic, more like a "Come as you are." When I was five I re-mem-ber my moth-er dug ear-rings out of the car. I knew that they were-n't hers, but it was-n't some-thing you'd wan-na dis-cuss. He was-n't warm, *Well, not to her ... well, not to us!* But

ev-'ry-thing was beau-ti-ful at the
ev-'ry-one was beau-ti-ful at the

bal-let. Grace-ful men lift love-ly girls in white. Yes,
bal-let. Ev-'ry prince has got to have his swan. Yes,

ev-'ry-thing was beau-ti-ful at the bal-let, hey! I was hap-py
ev-'ry-one is beau-ti-ful at the bal-let, hey! I was pret-ty

at the bal-let.
at the bal-let.

Up a steep and ver-y nar-row stair-way

to the voice like a met-ro-nome. Up a steep and ver-y nar-row stair-way, it

SING!
From the Joseph Papp Production of Michael Bennett's "A CHORUS LINE"

Music by MARVIN HAMLISCH
Lyric by EDWARD KLEBAN

THE MUSIC AND THE MIRROR

From the Joseph Papp Production of Michael Bennett's "A CHORUS LINE"

Music by MARVIN HAMLISCH
Lyric by EDWARD KLEBAN

Coda

Play— me the mu-sic, Play— me the mu-sic, Play— me the mu-sic.

Give me a chance— to come through. All I ev-er need-

ed was the mu - sic and the mir - ror and the chance—

to dance— for you.—

From the Joseph Papp Production of Michael Bennett's "A CHORUS LINE"

HELLO TWELVE, HELLO THIRTEEN, HELLO LOVE

Music by MARVIN HAMLISCH
Lyric by EDWARD KLEBAN

Hel - lo Twelve, Hel - lo Thir - teen, Hel - lo Love.— Chang - es,

Oh! down be - low, up a - bove.— Time to doubt, to break out,— it's a mess.—

(It's a mess.—) Time to grow— time to go— ad - o - lesce.— (Ad - o - lesce.—)

Too young— to take o - ver, too old— to ig-nore.—

Gee, I'm al-most read - y, *but what for?* There's a lot— I am not— cer-tain

of. Hel - lo Twelve,— Hel - lo Thir - teen, Hel - lo Love.—

DANCE: TEN; LOOKS: THREE

Music by MARVIN HAMLISCH
Lyric by EDWARD KLEBAN

ONE

Lyric by EDWARD KLEBAN
Music by MARVIN HAMLISCH

WHAT I DID FOR LOVE

Music by MARVIN HAMLISCH
Lyric by EDWARD KLEBAN